Books by David Melton

TODD
I'LL SHOW YOU THE MORNING SUN
JUDY, A REMEMBRANCE

A REMEMBRANCE

written and illustrated by

DAVID MELTON

STANYAN BOOKS

RANDOM HOUSE

A Stanyan book
Published by Stanyan Books,
8721 Sunset Blvd., Suite C
Hollywood, California 90069,
and by Random House, Inc.
201 East 50th Street,
New York, N.Y. 10022

L.C.#: 76-182688

ISBN: 0-394-48062-7

Printed in U.S.A.

Designed by David Melton

For Liza

INTRODUCTION

JUDY was a variety of colors and a multitude of moods. She came to maturity in the artificial light of vaudeville stages and Hollywood studios.

Her voice was clear and natural. She could elevate the emotional range of a song by revealing its simplest form. She could convey the meaning of a song in personal terms — a skill attained by only a handful of performers — Sinatra, for one, McKuen, for another.

She underlined humor with sly inflections, and could spit out tongue-twisting lyrics in diminishing chords for the fun of it all. But she always remained true to the song's intent. She believed her songs. And why not? They were hers for the taking.

There may never be another performer exactly like Judy, for there may never be another audience exactly like hers. Hers was an audience that grew out of the Depression and the War years, unashamed to be sentimental and romantic, or even patriotic. It was an audience of innocents, or at least, one which could still reflect on the loss of innocence. Perhaps she became a symbol of this loss, and the change which was taking place.

While columnists flashed her name in headlines and fan magazines perpetuated morbid sagas to exploit the tragedies of her life, Judy somehow retained her sense of humor and set her sights toward new triumphs.

In years to come, there will be many biographies of the legend which will claim to be the essence of the girl and the woman. There will be biographies of the woman which will claim to be the legend. As fact becomes more confused with fiction, supposition will propose to be reality, and reality will become illusion—and the legend will become legend.

— David Melton

Judy was a singer of songs
and a teller of stories.
She willingly shared
all that was hers to give,
and what was hers to give
was worth the sharing.

JUDY GARLAND

her life and her legend

Once upon a time,
in a valley of perpetual sunshine,
there was a land of make believe.
In the mythical kingdom of Hollywood,
kings and queens were not born —
they were invented —

Clark and Marilyn,
Myrna and Robert,
Joan and Gary,
and there was a little girl
called Judy.

On June 10, 1922, Frances Ethel Gumm was born to a family of vaudeville troupers. At the age of three, she made her stage debut singing "Jingle Bells" to an amateur night audience.

It was a beautiful land
of happy endings
and dreams come true,
of talented troupers
and carnival hustlers,
of high finance
and lowering standards,
of liquid stimulants
and sleeping pills.

In 1935, Louis B. Mayer, the head of MGM Studios, auditioned the plump thirteen-year-old singer and signed her to a contract. Frances Ethel Gumm became Judy Garland. She co-starred in a two-reel short, EVERY SUNDAY, with another young singer, Deanna Durbin. In BROADWAY MELODY OF 1938, Judy sang "Dear Mr. Gable," (YOU MADE ME LOVE YOU) to a photograph of "The King."

While the moguls
subdivided the kingdom
into higher and lower monarchies,
Judy sang of rainbows
and happy days,
of young girls' thoughts,
and young girl's hopes.

Her life was to take
more turns than
the yellow brick road,
and in time, her voice
would reflect fading rainbows
and shattered dreams.

As Dorothy Gale in the film classic, THE WIZARD OF OZ, Judy was established as a star. She was presented a special Academy Award for her performance, and the song "Over the Rainbow" became her trademark.

In the dreamworld

that was Hollywood

she learned to pretend –

she was the girl

who lived next door

to the boy next door.

She was first cast with Mickey Rooney in THOROUGHBREDS DON'T CRY in 1937 and was later teamed with her energetic friend in eight other films.

Tinsel was strung
against the backdrops
of sound stages.
Dimple-kneed darlings
descended spiral staircases
as heavenly choirs
chorused Berlin tunes.

Electric stars
and instant sentiment
became encased
in celluloid frames.

In the 1941 release, ZIEGFELD GIRL, Judy's exuberant talent held its share of the spotlight with the glamorous Hedy Lamarr and Lana Turner. Her rendition of the torrid tropical tune, "Minnie from Trinidad," brought raves from audiences and critics alike.

The songs were reminders
of other times
and other places,
of backstage hoofers
and on-stage clichés.

Vaudeville was remembered.

In films, MISS NELLY KELLY and FOR ME AND MY GAL, Judy graduated to adult roles, and shared the billing with George Murphy and Gene Kelly. Not only did she project a winning personality, but she began to establish herself as an actress.

Judy's voice
made the songs
ring fresh and new,
and when the
brown-eyed girl laughed,
audiences believed her laughter
and they loved her.

PRESENTING LILLY MARS, presented polished performances from both Judy and Van Heflin. Although she appeared to be a bright and happy girl on screen, the demanding studio schedules became a threat to her health.

It was a technicolor St. Louis—
the milkman delivered painted bottles
as the trolley rattled
across sound stages.
Halloween came from Booth Tarkington,
and Christmas drifted plastic snow.
The turn of the century
turned again,
then faded from view.

St. Louis doesn't live there anymore.

MEET ME IN ST. LOUIS revealed a thin-faced Judy, which pleased the studio head, but concerned her fans. However, the film became one of the biggest financial successes in MGM's history and provided Judy with a milestone in her ascending career.

Love came to the girl
in fragile packages.
Sometimes strings were tied
to the ribbons.

If love could not
endure endless schedules
and artificial lights,
how was the girl
expected to survive?

THE CLOCK, co-starring Robert Walker, gave Judy the opportunity of a straight dramatic role, proving her ability as a sensitive actress. Judy's marriages and her career would not share equal success. She was to marry orchestra leader and composer David Rose, director Vincente Minnelli, business manager Sid Luft, Mark Herron and Mickey Deans.

Chasing rainbows
and looking for silver linings
are children's games.
Where did dreams end
and the nightmares begin?

What did the camera care
about sleepless nights
and invading doubts?

Rigorous dieting didn't reduce Judy's performances in THE HARVEY GIRLS and EASTER PARADE, but the danger signals were posted. She was on the road to nervous exhaustion.

See the circus.
Hear the laughter.
Watch the funny clowns.
Hold tight to the brass ring
as the carousel
goes around,
and around,
and around,
and around.

Teaming with Gene Kelly in THE PIRATE and Fred Astaire in EASTER PARADE would bring some of Judy's brightest musical moments, but the rigorous routines posed additional physical strain.

Even the Emerald City
loses its luster.

And sometimes,
a little girl becomes lost
within the image
of the woman.

In a series of three cameo roles — ZIEGFELD FOLLIES, TILL THE CLOUDS ROLL BY, and WORDS AND MUSIC, a sophisticated Judy was displayed. Her satirical exposé of a glamorous actress in the classic "The Interview" pleased the critics and entertained her fans, but both wondered what had happened to the happy girl they remembered.

What do friendly stars
know of diet pills?
What do spotlights
know of shades of grey?

Even dream factories
discard illusions
for the reality
of dollars.

The frantic pace became too much. In 1949, she was suspended from the studio for missing rehearsals and was hospitalized in nervous exhaustion. A plump round-faced Judy returned to the screen, and the studio brass demanded new thin-down campaigns. Judy sang "Get Happy" but its lyric could not have been farther from the truth. SUMMER STOCK was her last film for MGM and there were rumors that her career was finished.

But the voice
was no illusion
and the talent
was no dream
that could be
turned off
like a kleiglight.

Courage cannot
be bought or sold.

In 1951, earning $20,000 a week at the London Palladium, Judy proved that her special magic could transcend beyond the sound stages, and that her talent was larger than the silver screen.

And who determined
that coming home
should be called
a "comeback"?

Didn't they know
that palaces
were built
for royalty?

Following her triumph at the Palladium,
Judy revived vaudeville's two-a-day at New York's
Palace Theatre. Breaking all box office records,
her four-week engagement was extended
into a nineteen-week run— the longest continuing
headline billed at the famous theater.

Lights!
Camera!
Action!
Close up.

Watch closely.
See how it's done.

Cinemascope
wasn't wide enough
to contain the magic.

Technicolor
wasn't bright enough
to project
the range of the colors.

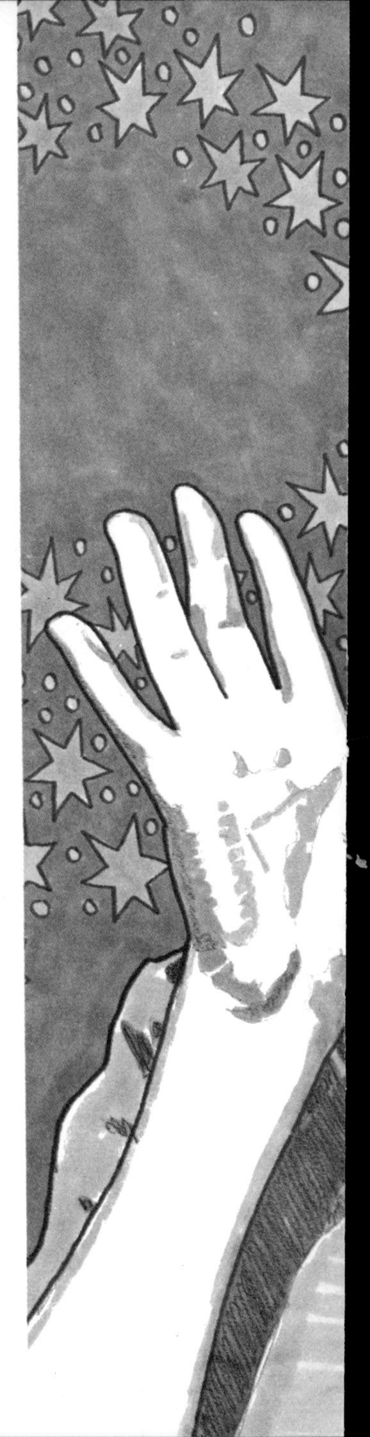

Judy's new power as a singer and skill as an actress provided a one-woman tour de force in the 1954 release of A STAR IS BORN.

The woman knows
the performer,
and the performer
knows the rhythms.

They became one —
the woman,
the performer.
Together,
they became legend.

A STAR IS BORN was a critical success and Judy was nominated for an Academy Award for her performance. Before general release, forty minutes were slashed from the film, deleting two of the production numbers and many of the early motivation scenes. Still, what remained is considered to be classic.

Where does a legend live?
What street can it call its own?
It can't be contained in one house
or in a single room.

After the release of A STAR IS BORN, Judy returned to concert and nightclub commitments. Marital, emotional, and financial crises plagued her.

Legends don't live in buildings.
They are a part of the senses.
Legends are of the mind
and of the heart.

After a six-year absence from the screen, Judy returned in 1961 in a small but key role in JUDGMENT AT NUREMBERG and was promptly nominated for an Academy Award as Best Supporting Actress of the Year. Her next film was also a straight dramatic role with Burt Lancaster in A CHILD IS WAITING.

The overture builds
to new excitements.
A spotlight slashes
through the starless night
to encircle the face of a legend.
The voice caresses the audience
and holds it captive.

On April 29, 1961, a star-studded audience assembled to hear Judy sing at Carnegie Hall. It became a happening. Her voice was never better, her timing never keener—she was in perfect form. "I'll stay and sing all night," she told her audience and they were more than willing to stay with her. Recordings of the performances sold into the millions.

Never look back
at the fragile past.
Take the here,
hold on to the now,
and live for today.

In 1962, Judy starred in what was to be her last film — I COULD GO ON SINGING. The film did not measure up to the power of her performance.

Cameras are all the same.
They are mechanical robbers
of sensitive illusions.
They take away
and give back
so little in return.

Having appeared in two highly successful television specials, THE FORD STAR JUBILEE in 1955, and THE JUDY GARLAND SHOW in 1963, Judy signed with CBS for an ill-fated weekly musical variety series premiered in September of 1963. The show came alive only when Judy was allowed to do her thing—sing. In the last few shows of the series, she took the stage and spent the entire hour in concert, proving what had been missing. But it was too late; the show was cancelled.

Although the legend
was often projected
in shades
of melancholy blue,
the woman,
somehow,
retained her sense of humor.

Concerts became her greatest triumphs. At the Palladium, she shared the stage with her daughter, Liza Minnelli. Liza's talents made it clear that her mother had built more than a legend—she was also to leave a legacy.
Later, in a return engagement at the Palace, her other two children, Lorna and Joey Luft, appeared with her.

The charisma that was Judy's
did not diminish;
instead it expanded.
The upbeat set feet tapping
to exciting rhythms.
The downbeat moved
even the most
sophisticated audience to tears.
For when the spotlight
narrowed to Judy's childlike face,
audiences were reminded
of rainbows
and a little girl
who long ago
stole their hearts.

In August 1967, Judy Garland returned to Broadway and to the Palace Theatre for the last time. A dangerously thin Judy, clad in a copper-toned sequined pantsuit, entered through the lobby and greeted her audience as she hurried down the aisle to take her place on the stage. She not only sang to her audience, but she talked with them.
At the closing of the opening night performance, the standing ovation lasted for 25 minutes. Without knowing, it was her last goodbye.

On June 22, 1969,
Judy Garland was dead.

Although she is gone,
there is a legacy
of 36 films,
and hours of splendid recordings.

Orson Welles once wrote,
"The true importance of an artist
is judged, not by how much he
impresses us, but by the gifts
we receive from him."

Judy's gift to the world
was hours of sheer entertainment.
It was, indeed, a precious gift;
one to be treasured and remembered.